OUTSOURCING

Build great company with

outsourced team, work

less and earn more

1. Introduction

The present economic scenario does not allow businesses much leeway in terms of investment, productivity, and profits. Globalization has brought in a high level of competitiveness making it necessary for businesses to look to smarter ways of doing business.

The concept of retiring at 60 has become obsolete now. With smart outsourcing strategies, it is possible to reap huge benefits with minimal effort. The new trend in financial freedom is automation of business with outsourcing. Outsourcing is the ideal way to earn big money passively, while you continue focusing on your core business. Outsourcing is not a new trend. The concept has been used with success for more than thousand years.

The difference is, it has increased in popularity now. In simple terms, outsourcing is getting your work done via a third party seller on contractual terms. While you may be able to still complete the work on your own, outsourcing helps cutting down costs, which is the key reason for businesses world over opting for the business strategy.

At present reducing overheads is not the only benefit received from outsourcing. It has a wide array of benefits including flexible staffing, better skilled expertise, more efficiency, and low turnaround time. All these benefits eventually end up in the business generating higher returns, which is what every business aims at. Just as in any business, you venture into outsourcing also needs proper research and planning. When you find a good outsourcing partner or team, you will be able to focus on your business in the best way possible and gain competitive advantage easily.

Statistics on various outsourcing models reveal that it is indeed the best and most competitive long-term strategy to succeed in business. This eBook on outsourcing is a comprehensive guide for startups. The immense amount of info provided in this guide aims at motivating a business owner towards automation via outsourcing, generating passive income and with less effort too.

With a great outsourcing strategy, business owners can work fewer hours in a week and still manage to earn an appreciable profit, while they take care of their core business.

This book will guide the reader on outsourcing including actual product and online business, examples of outsourcing, places to outsource, managing the outsourcing business and other relevant and crucial information needed to make outsourcing an effective one.

With the ideas, motivation, and guidance provided in this book, a startup will be able to establish its business solidly, with able support of its outsourcing team leaving behind sufficient time to focus on the priorities and best of all live a relaxed and prosperous life. Welcome to the world of outsourcing!

2. Outsourcing -a brief overview

Before you embark on the ways and means to accomplish setting up an outsourcing team, here is a short overview on outsourcing, which will help you understand about it better and utilize it more effectively.

Evolution of Outsourcing

Outsourcing emerged as a viable business concept in the wake of the Industrial Revolution when companies started to look into the avenues, which would let them gain competitive edge in the market and increase their profits.

During the twentieth century, the business model that prevailed involved processes, which manage, own and directly wield control over the assets of the business.

During the 1960s and 1970s, the focus turned on diversification of businesses and taking advantage of the scaling up of the business economy. While globalization yielded profits, the diversification required an equally diversified management prowess. This led to reduced agility because of the bloated management system.

Businesses needed to become more flexible and creative. At such a critical time, outsourcing became a strong beacon beckoning the companies to identify critical aspects of their business that were outsourceable, so they can focus on their core process without unnecessary distractions.

Outsourcing as an ideal business strategy

Businesses started to accept the feasibility of outsourcing in the early 1990s only. Even before that, businesses were not completely self-sufficient. Outsourcing was used in areas of the business in which they lacked competence.

For instance, publishers outsourced printing, composition and fulfillment, which were essential services that they did not possess internal expertise for. Since these are ancillary but essential services, outsourcing soon started to transform from being the exception to the norm.

Slowly businesses started considering use of outsourcing for their support services. The cost saving trend in organizations in the 1990s forced companies to outsource most of the services required for managing a company except the core business process.

Accounting, data processing, human resources, security, distribution of internal mail, maintenance of industrial plant and other related housekeeping tasks were taken care of with outsourcing. This enabled improved finances for businesses, as they were able to cut down costs in the important functions.

Tactical collaboration

Initially, outsourcing was considered only for the peripheral services and not the core business functions, which give strategic edge to the company and make it unique. Core functions of a company also relate to those that get the company closer to its customers.

The decision of Eastman Kodak to outsource its IT systems, which were vital for its business in 1989, was an out- of- the -box, radical move, but one which paid back phenomenally for the company. Following this success formula, several big corporations decided that outsourcing technology was a better proposition than owning it.

Thus, the present business trend does not rest on ownership, but on forming tactical collaborations to get a more enhanced yield. Hence, outsourcing has become the norm, where it is not based on the commodity or core function, but on which outsourcing process can deliver the best result.

Defining outsourcing

Outsourcing is the strategic utilization of resources from outside to take care of activities that were conventionally handled by the internal resources and staff of a business. Outsourcing is a form of business automation where all major functions are taken care of by efficient and specialized service providers and they are in effect valued partners of the business.

Hiring contractors to take care of certain tasks in a business is a common practice. This helps to even the workload and form good long-term connections with firms that offer complementary or supplementary services.

But outsourcing differs from this simple subcontracting in the need for substantial restructuring of the business activities. This includes staff transfer from the host business to the outsourcing specialist that has the required core skills.

Why companies outsource

Outsourcing is chosen by companies to meet with the changing strategic needs of their business. Asset transfer, superior capability, best use of resources, better ROI and mitigation of risks are salient points that make companies strongly support outsourcing.

Lower wages is one big decisive factor for outsourcing. For instance, security services when outsourced are far cheaper, when compared to use of in house security as these people had wages equal to the skilled factory workers.

There are several reasons as to why companies decide on outsourcing. Here are a few of them:

- Cut down operating costs
- To compensate for insufficient internal resources
- To take care of functions that are time consuming and difficult to manage and control
- Facilitate company to focus on its core objectives
- Utilize globalized and expert services
- Open up internal resources enabling better use of them

- Share business risks with a partner establishment

While earlier businesses sought outsourcing to reduce overheads and employee count, now outsourcing has far more strategic implications. Businesses use outsourcing for value adding functions of the company, so the core competencies are utilized in the best manner possible.

In-depth Involvement

While outsourcing may seem to be simple at the outset, it has several factors that can affect the success of the venture. The business should have a clear understanding of its objectives and goals, create a tactical vision, and chart a plan accordingly. Selection of the right outsourcing company is the next step in the process. Once selection is done, a solid contract structure should be created.

Simple signing of outsourcing agreement is not the end of your responsibility for ensuring success. Statistics reveal that lack of proper attention to the critical details can make the outsourcing contract unviable and lead to its cancellation. To ensure effective outsourcing, the senior management should pitch in and help with the contract implementation.

The entire operational level taskforce should be involved in executing the implementation of outsourcing. This ensures that all probable issues are identified and resolved, guaranteeing continued satisfaction all around.

A viable agreement at the service level should be made available to the employees concerned with the outsourcing. Open communication with the groups or individuals affected by the outsourcing and management of the new partnership should be executed smoothly.

The internal environment should be handled with care by involving the senior executives and getting their full support. Financial justification and proper attention to personnel problems should be taken care of meticulously to make the outsourcing an all-round success.

Deciding on outsourcing

Making the decision on in-house service over outsourcing does not have any simple formula. It would augur well for a business, if each project is assessed based on its specific merits, as outsourcing has numerous benefits that can turn around the business profitably.

In most cases, outsourcing is strongly favored, as it would help cut down operational costs. With the decision to outsource, a business has an increased chance of becoming effective, efficient, and flexible with an accompanying cost reduction. This certainly tips the scales in favor of outsourcing. Here are some important pros of using outsourcing

• Flexibility in staffing
• Faster turnaround and time to market
• Business operations comes under care of expert professionals
• Best practice application capability
• Permanent staff gains more knowledge
• Predictable and cost effective expenses
• Creative and flexible problem solving experts at the company's disposal
• Focus on core competence and resources

The outsourcing process

Any outsourcing process has four phases namely,

1. Program initiation: This is the beginning phase of outsourcing where a business evaluates various opinions and concepts about the advantage of the program, its results, and execution. The initiation phase utilizes the concepts and purposes and documents them in a contract draft form.

2. Service implementation: This phase involves actions taken to make the purposes and concepts a reality. These are developed further into a planned and formal program of outsourcing and transitioned to the actual outsourcing service including transition project definition, staff transfer, Service Level Agreement and service reporting, implementing and transfer of service and implementation of processes in managing the service.

This phase is critical because continuity should be maintained after the outsourcing service providers take over. The deadlines, timescales, and quality of the service should be intact during this transition phase.

3. Final Agreement: Amendments are made to the contract draft drawn in the initiation phase and final contract is completed after the end of negotiations.

4. Program closure: A formal closure of the program is necessary to receive the maximum advantage. The new change should be accepted by the staff and the management, and they should move forward positively to ensure success. The information collected during the program period will have to be formally recorded for reference in future.

Outsourcing for startups can create a phenomenal shift in the way the business is operated. While many copy the existing successful models, an effective outsourcing strategy can be arrived at only when the best practices are implemented with appropriate strategic rational.

With outsourcing, companies can limit the overspending and boost their profitability. It is a valuable strategy, which is useful for companies that want to limit their scope in their present value chain and for companies who want to expand their services in an industry value level. Outsourcing is an ideal way to build value chains with its lucrative operations strategy that can be applied across a diverse range of industries with measurable success.

3. Why outsourcing is profitable for businesses

Startups as well as established businesses would definitely benefit from the flexibility and passive income that outsourcing is capable of, provided the positive and negative aspect of the strategy are considered well. Even when you consider the drawbacks in outsourcing, the benefits outweigh the risks considerably.

When you take care to streamline the company objectives, employee welfare and the reason for outsourcing, you are sure to see huge profits you had never imagined with your startup. This chapter will enumerate on the various reasons as to why outsourcing is profitable for your startup.

Prioritize core business functions

Before outsourcing arrived with a bang in the business world, companies had to contend with all aspects of their business irrespective of their level of importance. This required plenty of resources and time.

For instance, a health care institution would have to take care of non-core aspects such as medical billing, claims processing, transcription etc. which can dilute the focus needed for the actual core health care.

Increased workload and low quality work in the core function becomes the norm. This can reduce productivity and put your business in peril, if it is not dealt with properly. But with outsourcing, such functions can be taken care of without loss of resources, both human and money related and save time too.

Boost internal efficiency

By making use of third party external outsourcing companies, you can ensure freeing of internal resources of your organization, which is vital for taking care of mission centric activities.

Once tasks are allocated to the outsourcing partner, the workload on your employees is reduced. This will help them work efficiently and you can develop your task force in a better way.

Embrace latest trends

With new technologies being introduced continuously, businesses should take advantage of them as these pave the way for better investment management, quality and productivity. Outsourcing comes in handy in such a situation.

Instead of spending time and resources on acquiring the new technologies, outsourcing such technologies will help in shifting to the new technology with minimal disruption in productivity and downtime.

Better risk mitigation

When you outsource tasks, any associated risks will be shared by the outsourcing partner. This will reduce your burden considerably. For instance, the risks of failure are much reduced, when you outsource a special task, instead of having the task done by in house people who do not have the required expertise for the job.

An outsourcing partner in any situation helps supplement the company's operations with adequate backup processes and redundancies. In case of accidents, natural calamities, technical crisis, or fluctuation in the markets, the outsourcing helps in fast, efficient, and rigorous recovery processes.

Thus, the company will respond immediately and get the situation under control in no time at all. This will put less stress on the expenses and increase profitability.

Invest less in infrastructure

By removing many of the functions outside the company, you can reduce the expenses made on infrastructure for executing these functions. Technical support, call center equipment, and sophisticated IT infrastructure can take up a huge part of your investment. When you outsource these functions, and external vendors takeover the operation, it is possible to make a very low investment in such areas.

Enhance capability

While financial benefits are the foremost consideration in opting for outsourcing, access to superior capabilities is another important reason for businesses. Since operational expertise in all aspects of a business is necessary for profitability, but not a feasible option financially, outsourcing helps to possess expertise without having to own it. Superior infrastructure and capabilities can hence be accessed without spending huge amounts on them.

Operational performance is also enhanced, when a company outsources to vendors having domain expertise in the specific process outsourced to them. The vendor experience enables better operational efficiency for the company outsourcing the process.

Save big

Saving money on expenditure in terms of labor, infrastructure, and other resources is a key reason for the popularity of outsourcing. Many western firms outsource to Asian countries like India, Philippines, and China etc. due to the low labor cost there. The quality of the outsourced processes is also similar to the donor region. Hence, this would result in huge cost savings. Costs related to HR, administrative costs, payroll, rentals, utilities, and power are also saved due to the outsourcing.

Infrastructure maintenance is an additional burden, which outsourcing eliminates efficiently. With a trusted vendor, outsourcing helps save on the efforts put in by your business personnel, time and capital expenditure. Further, with outsourcing it is no longer necessary to spend on resources such as training employees, buying costly software or spending big money on the latest technologies. This results in better returns, when you consider the long-term effects.

Flexible operations

When independent tasks are outsourced, it enables the business to have flexibility at the financial level, especially when there is demand uncertainty. Scaling down or up can be done without fear of repercussions. With off shore outsourcing, you get the additional benefit of managing the business capably even during the holidays and season timings, when the operations slow down normally.

In the UK and US for instance, during off-season time and during the holidays there is an acute shortage of workers. When the companies outsource from Asian countries like India, they are able to compensate for the deficient staff during holiday season.

Further shortage of talent is another reason for companies to outsource the talent. When the yesteryear workers approach their retirement, it is difficult to substitute their skills with fresh talent. Finding new comers with identical skills is not easy. making it necessary to search for the talent elsewhere. Outsourcing helps fill in this gap effectively.

Round the clock operations

When you outsource to a location that experiences a time zone that is different from the location you are in, it is possible to utilize a 24-hour day to the maximum. This is especially useful, when you require completion of critical tasks in a short turnaround time.

The work will be continuing while you are asleep and will be waiting for review, when you start work the following day. This way you will increase overall productivity. Further, you will be able to provide 24/7 customer support, when you make use of offshore outsourcing.

Make your business customer centric

The skills you acquire with the help of outsourcing will result in faster deliverables of top quality boosting the turnaround time considerably. You can provide guaranteed customer satisfaction with the high quality service and on time delivery of services. This would increase the number of loyal customers and make you well established.

Maintain competitive edge

Sometimes businesses need the use of applications just for a single time. They would have to spend a huge amount of resources to set up such an application and benefit from it. Such ad hoc applications can be utilized without having to spend money on them by outsourcing. This leads to better competitive advantage, which is the objective of any business.

With strategic outsourcing you can

•   Provide exemplary service to your customer

•   Increase productivity

•   Manage your resources smartly

When your competitors have not yet realized the true potential of outsourcing, you can surpass them easily and set new standards in productivity, reaching your goal of passive income much earlier than you had envisioned.

4. Various outsourcing segments

When you aim at having an uninterrupted access to state of the art technology and best practices in the industry, the best and only way to accomplish it is by outsourcing. You can take advantage of the economy of scale of the outsourcing company, refrain from investing in highly trained personnel, while you focus on your core business activities. Outsourcing can be done in almost all aspects of a business except the core segments. Here are some commonly outsourced services:

I.   **Professional outsourcing**

This outsourcing category includes specialized services such as accounting, information technology, administrative support, financial and others. This is a commonly outsourced category as the cost savings with this service is very high. You need to pay for the provided services, but you can gain access to top quality resources, which brings down the overhead costs remarkably. The various subcategories include,

Finance: Auditing is mostly outsourced. Other areas that can be outsourced as easily include tax management, invoicing, bookkeeping, and other accounting functions.

Health and security: You can outsource consultants specializing in compliance of safety and health jobs. With their assistance, you can meet with the stringent safety rules, especially in case of tasks that have complicated risks. In addition, this can be done in a more cost effective way than when you do it on your own.

Marketing and sales: You can outsource marketing communications and sales to an outsourcing agency or consultant. Small businesses especially find outsourcing of this type profitable.

HR and Business process: This includes outsourcing activities including payroll, recruitment, secretarial services, and recruitment. You get access to specialist talents but you have to pay only when you use the services.

II. Personal virtual assistant outsourcing services

Outsourcing a personal assistant or virtual assistant is one important outsourcing service that any business would benefit from. A virtual personal assistant can help lighten your task load, organize your daily tasks, and let you focus on your business in a better way. You will have quite a lot to handle as a business owner, seeing to the set up and growth of the business. Completing routines tasks or the long lists at hand can eat up your precious time. You can outsource these tasks to remote efficient workers who can complete a wide range of tasks from administrative work to personal tasks. You can be more organized and productive this way and the cost is much lower than hiring an employee full time.

Some of the tasks a virtual assistant can take care of include

Office tasks

Clean mail inbox by creating rules, filters and answering unimportant emails.

Send alerts on the important emails

Use rules and templates for inquiries on customer service

Set up schedule for the following day meetings with appropriate dossiers

Set up meetings every week by corresponding with co-workers

Issue alerts on upcoming events and other things that need to be taken action on

Coordinate travel including flight planning, finding restaurants for client meetings and create itinerary for trips.

Take care of copywriting and marketing tasks.

Research

A virtual assistant helps in gathering information on technology, find out networking events, create client or contact dossiers, organize contacts' details, sort CRM information, track purchases from the website, and graph them.

Social media assistance

Taking care of social activities online is critical for businesses to stay up to date and gain a competitive edge. A virtual assistant helps in tasks such as update social media profile, assist in fundable or Kickstarter campaign, schedule blog posts and social media, schedule tweets and other social media activities.

Personal tasks

Tasks of personal nature are also adeptly handled by virtual personal assistants. They research and purchase gifts for family and friends during holiday season, set up appointments with hair stylist, dentist, doctors, and handle other such appointments. They can find appropriate activities for children and update their schedule, purchase, and delivery of groceries and meals, household items etc., schedule home cleaning, meal planning and pay receipts and bills,.

Virtual assistants also help in achieving your personal goals by keeping you motivated and accountable. They find resources that keep you right on track and set up reward system for milestones.

III.   IT outsourcing

Outsourcing IT services is a popular way used by businesses to utilize technology rich resources. Either part or the entire information technology services are outsourced. Functions such as project work, data warehousing, website development etc. can be done with the aid of groundbreaking technology and latest upgrades with outsourcing. This will not involve buying expensive systems or keeping track of industry trends.

Functions such as software development, support, and maintenance too are taken care of via outsourcing. Since all businesses have IT requirements and deal with IT at some level, this outsourcing category is used commonly.

The outsourcing is considered profitable as the skills and infrastructure needed for forming an in-house team is very expensive, when compared to contracting the work to a skilled third party vendor.

IT outsourcing is also done, when a company cannot afford the expense or is not willing to maintain data storage systems. This applies to medium and small-scale organizations. For large-scale businesses, IT outsourcing is done in segments only.

The advantage of outsourcing IT services is the ability of the service relationship to continue irrespective of the location of the IT provider. There are two types of IT outsourcing:

External Domestic outsourcing

This is also known as baseline outsourcing stage. With this type of outsourcing, companies strike a relationship with a domestic outsourcing provider. The outsourcing of technology services by Kodak to IBM in the year 1989 can be classified under this category.

External international outsourcing

 This is more prevalent now, as there are several external IT outsourcing services at the international level. With the internet and cost effective communications present now, this type of outsourcing has become a viable option. You can transfer IT activities to any place in the world.

IV.   Manufacturer outsourcing

Outsourcing in the manufacturing industry was popularized in the United States during the beginning of 21st Century. Blue-collar tasks were taken over by third party vendors for reasons such as

- Work expertise
- Human investment
- Cost factors
- Time to market

Since then the concept has moved on to white-collar employment for the very same reasons. The outsourcing in the manufacturing segment is industry specific. For instance, an automobile maker can outsource the design and manufacture of windows for all the models they make. This would reduce time take for assembling the windows and save costs in a big way.

While outsourcing is cost efficient, it is important to ensure the quality is not compromised. Further, in case of the automobile window outsourcing, the task should not interfere or interrupt the production speed. Medium and small size manufacturers too need to use this type of outsourcing to keep up with the competition. Since such companies do not have scalable economies, it is difficult for them to compete with their larger counterparts who are able to invest in upgradation of equipment, processes, and personnel. As the market sees a constant shrinking of product lifecycles, it is necessary for small and medium scale companies to embrace this outsourcing segment, so they can survive and prosper.

IV.   Multi-sourcing

Multisourcing is a recently evolved segment in outsourcing involving IT. Any business aspect can benefit from outsourcing although it is mostly used in relation to IT outsourcing. Multisourcing is a blend of IT services and business derived from a chief set of external and internal providers, to reach business objectives. Introduced in 2005, multisourcing is used frequently by large organizations, which require multiple vendors to take care of the IT infrastructure and operations.

Multisourcing is popular as it uses the best of the specialist teams to focus on a main management feature in IT. The strategy is outcome based and functions based on partner relationship. The advantages of this approach include better knowledge about the real status of the project and minimal disruptions in the various functions. When you use multisourcing, you need to have

- A proper strategy for sourcing
- Network of relationship
- Good governance
- Create meaningful measurements

While outsourcing is a big boon to businesses, when done compulsively without proper consideration, evaluation and benchmarking of the impact on the business, it can fail to give the desired results.

Instead of outsourcing a single function or operation, which is becoming ineffective fast in the present day complicated business set up, multisourcing can help to streamline services both externally and internally with proper evaluation of the efficiency and effectiveness. Multisourcing is a revolutionary strategy that is not just an improved form of outsourcing. It empowers organizations with the capability of global expansion, profitability, competitive advantage and higher agility.

Due to its complex functions, outsourcing needs a new framework and approach for communication, interaction, and monitoring of the service relationship internally and externally. With mulitsourcing, you can easily drive your startup to become a leading player in the industry in future.

V.   Specific process outsourcing

Outsourcing is termed as specific process, when the services belong to a specific internal procedure. At present, companies routinely, resort to this type of outsourcing. For instance, a confectionary can outsource package delivery of its sweets to courier companies such as FedEx or UPS.

This type of contract for outsourcing involves delivery timelines, costs, customer contact etc. By taking care of such functions with outsourcing, the company can focus on its core strength and boost customer service, while reducing the time and cost involved in doing the work on its own,

Process outsourcing also denotes outsourcing control of services in the public sector like armed forces, fire, police, etc. to appropriate for-profit organizations.

VI.   Near shoring

Nearshoring is a rapidly growing outsourcing strategy in recent times. It is a combined form of reshoring and offshoring. In nearshoring, the outsourcing company chooses an outsourcing provider present nearer to the economic structure or time zone of its home country. This reduces overheads and boosts services.

Hence countries like the US outsource to Latin American countries such as Columbia, Chile and Costa Rica. This is because of the proximity of these countries to the US and the nearer time zone. Faster speed to market, reduced costs, and convenient business operations because of shorter travel time, and fewer hours of working late are some of the chief advantages of nearshoring that businesses cannot afford to ignore.

However, the outsourced countries such as Argentina, Brazil, and Mexico need to address social, economic, and political risks they present, which can jeopardize the nearshoring operation. With the change in market trends, technology, economy, labor and oil costs, businesses should look to make the necessary changes in their outsourcing strategies.

VII.   Reshoring

In the past few decades, many US companies had outsourced their manufacturing jobs to countries such as India and China due to the low labor cost and infrastructure requirements. And this was considered as a smart move.

But, recently there is a shift in this approach, as the companies have started awakening to the fact that the outsourcing is not as profitable as they had thought. Now several companies are shifting their manufacturing functions from offshore location and moving the jobs to their home country. This is termed as reshoring. Reshoring in other words is an outsourcing process done in reverse. It entails transfer of the operations of a business back to the home country of the business. Reshoring has advantages such as reduced shipping costs. Rising oil costs has made shipping of the manufactured products an expensive one. Further, the custom charges, duties, and delays in shipping are major drawbacks of outsourcing that reshoring can reverse.

The downside of offshore outsourcing increases stress on cash flow and the cost of the manufactured goods for businesses and consumers. Some companies take this a step further and shift to insourcing. They bring back the outsourced services, which third party vendors had taken care of earlier to be handled by their company and this is achieved by vertical integration occasionally.

VIII. Offshore

Outsourcing as a concept was not much in use during the early twentieth and nineteenth centuries. Businesses did not think of outsourcing to a specialized or individual company out of their country. But, now outsourcing is commonplace and is thought of as a smart and revolutionary strategy.

Outsourcing enables companies to expand their business globally, capture new markets, and use talent, which is not available locally. Offshore outsourcing is also referred to as reshoring and nearshoring based on the outsourced location. Offshoring denotes outsourcing services to be done in another country. This was the first concept to become popular but later on nearshoring and reshoring became a norm. Offshoring is mainly preferred because of the low labor costs. It also enables making use of skills that is not available locally. Sometimes offshoring is considered beneficial, when certain activities are prohibited due to regulations in the native region.

China, India, and Indonesia are important countries considered for offshore outsourcing. The reason for Industries in the US and UK outsourcing to these countries is due to the massive telecommunication capability and the advent of internet in the 90s.

IX. BPO

Business process outsourcing (BPO) is a category of outsourcing that is used for outsourcing operational activities. This is more used in businesses with manufacturing base than other industries. This is because manufacturing businesses have specific operations, which are better done when outsourced.

For instance, repair and maintenance of machine is more cost effective when outsourced. Landscaping, cleaning, maintenance of facilities and property too come under operational activities, which can be outsourced effectively. Outsourcing enables the organization to cut down the expenses towards such activities. Other than manufacturing segment, BPO services deal with IT sector too. The services offered in this sector include transcription, content writing, web development, proofreading, editing, legal services, HR services, data entry, DTP, medical billing, business consulting, CAD, call centers, animation, book keeping, multimedia, financial etc.

X. KPO

KPO (Knowledge Process Outsourcing), which is an extension of BPO, deals with higher worker expertise. The outsourced work involves higher level of research, technical and analytical skills, and decisions made are of a complex and higher level than BPO services.

Some examples of this sector include simulation, patent research, pharmaceutical research etc. Data analysis, research, and development, database building, and content development are also included in the KPO services. It is mature than BPO services.

KPO services require specialized domain centric knowledge of higher level and include BPO, RPO (Research Process Outsourcing) and APO (Analysis Process Outsourcing). Instead of just providing process expertise, as in the other outsourcing categories, KPO deals with advanced analytical talent and expertise in business. Experience, judgement, and in-depth knowledge are needed in this outsourcing, while BPO is just about volume, efficiency, and size.

5. How to manage outsourcing without taking up your precious time

Most often businesses are under the misconception that once the contract on outsourcing is signed, they need not concern about it anymore. The fact is the contract signing is just the beginning of a relationship, which needs to be nurtured with care thereafter.

Whether you own a big or small business, when you plan to outsource different business tasks, you should decide on setting up a proper framework that helps manage the outsourcing process. Proper management is necessary, as it not only makes the outsourcing a successful one but also benefits the business in other ways. From selection of the appropriate provider, deal negotiation and relationship management to distribution, proper management is important for success of the outsourcing.

With the right management, the benefits a business receives include:

• Improved performance and work quality
• Better organization and coordination
• Improved crisis and risk management
• Reduction in overall expenditure
• Streamlined outsourcing process

What businesses should aim at?

To manage outsourcing processes successfully, your business needs proper communication channels, safe knowledge transfer systems and complete transparency as well as control. The first step towards achieving this is monitoring certain core functional aspects of the service provider and the client. Ignoring any specific area, leads to failure of the outsourcing process. The significant areas to focus on include:

Managing cost

Cost is a key reason for opting outsourcing, as it provides profit for both the service provider and the business. Hence, it is necessary to analyze the scope of outsourcing and pricing before the outsourcing is done.

Right communication

Establishing proper channels of communication is necessary for the success of the outsourcing irrespective of the type of outsourcing you decide on. Communication strategy should be followed with diligence right from when the deal is negotiated.

The communication system should be fool proof and consistent contact should be established between the concerned parties with regular feedback, instruction clarity and development of a proper system for clearing any issues in the process.

You need not resort to endless hours of training or elaborate document exchange to communicate the goals of your business, customers and employees to the outsourcing provider. You need to just share all these elements effectively to help them align with your goals and build real value.

When you create the atmosphere for a workflow that is robust and well designed, it will help create better accuracy and enhance effectiveness of the project. To communicate your specific needs all the written communication should be accompanied by visual aids, wireframes, and images. When you are specific, the chances of getting the results you aim at increases manifold. Further, the processes should have a proper tracking system to measure the productivity and quality.

Monitoring performance

This includes overseeing performance of the quality of the project and the upkeep of timelines as mentioned in the agreement. The business should conduct checks regularly on the quality standards. Respecting deadlines and accountability should also be present to ensure proper compliance.

Manage risks

Risk management is critical to ensure all the possible risks are minimized. The risks in relation to the business and outsourcing provider should be evaluated and a proper back up established before an agreement is signed.

Deal with crisis effectively

Since crisis can happen to the business or the outsourcing provider at any time, it is necessary for both parties to be prepared appropriately for crisis management. When a reputed outsourcing provider is selected, the crisis management efforts can be reduced substantially.

Transparency in management

To enable continuous transfer of knowledge in every area of the outsourced project in a transparent manner, you should monitor the process regularly. This will improve timelines, production, and the quality of the service you have outsourced.

Forge good relationship

For the outsourcing to progress smoothly without any hitches, it is vital to build good relationship with the outsourcing provider. This can be achieved with regular communication, transparency, and flexibility whenever and wherever needed. For a hassle free experience in outsourcing, here are some ways in which a sound relationship can be formed.

• Dedicated team for customer support available 24/7, providing assistance to sort out issues and answer queries

• Creating a working agreement that is transparent and clear in its terms in relation to Service Level Agreement and Non-Disclosure Agreement.

• Three tiered quality control process to maintain top quality throughout the project

- Stringent observance of deadlines, which avoids unnecessary delays
- Enforcing cost competitive structure for pricing to gain substantial profits

Setting up in-house team for management

Just as external management is critical to succeed in outsourcing, you should also focus on internal management, which involves taking care of the process within your business. To enforce in-house monitoring of the project, you need to train your employees in

•   Analysis of capability of the project depending on the demand and supply

•   Making appropriate decisions on workload distribution in offshore and in-house processes

•   Establish monitoring program to assess the quality of offshore outsourcing via surveys and assessment of reviews of the services.

•   Making pricing benchmarks to regulate prices

•   Including updated, cheaper, and smarter technology services by keeping constant contact with the market trends

6. Examples of commonly outsourced work

The previous chapter would have enlightened you on the various types of outsourcing segments in practice now. With globalization and the internet, you can see all types of business tasks being outsourced in an inexpensive but efficient way. Whether you are thinking of venturing into a small, medium or big business set up, outsourcing can help strengthen your business and make it more established.

At the outset, you may not be sure about the tasks, which you want to outsource, and whether they are effective. While experts may suggest that all tasks, except the core skill of your business be outsourced, this does not apply in all situations. Here are some examples of commonly outsourced jobs, so you can have a better understanding of the strategy.

Customer support

This is the most common task outsourced by all businesses. Phone support is the most frequently outsourced task. Since it is cost inhibitive to allocate space, training, and pay taxes on customer support set up, outsourcing the service to a country such as India is a viable option. The cost involved is just a fraction of the amount a business would spend in America. While this option is cost saving, it can also have drawbacks such as insufficient expertise and failure to understand issues.

Custom research analysis

This involves finding detailed solutions or answers to unique issues and queries consumers have such as gathering data on the startup weekend events and fairs happening in the upcoming weeks. It can also be a personal kind of research such as finding the day care options present near the office or home, or finding the best travel options for near and far destinations.

Accounting

This service is ideal for outsourcing. The standard methodology used helps in finding the best professionals at cost effective rates. With many professionals, being trained for accounting, outsourcing services it is convenient for countries like the United States to use their services to take care of bookkeeping and financial statements. But at the same time, since this is a critical part of any business, you should ensure that you select appropriate outsourcing service.

Taking care of taxes

Preparation of tax is similar to accounting in being a standard procedure. It is possible for a qualified outsourcing team to prepare tax return filings when the required financial receipts, income statements, ledgers, balance sheets, and other relevant details are provided.

But since this is a significant part of a business, you need to be selective when trusting company information with a third party. When you fail to choose the right team, it can result in errors, which can lead to unwanted and drastic consequences ranging from higher interest, penalties, or worse being audited.

Web designing

This is more of an artistic job and is one, which is often outsourced. You can find several well-qualified teams to choose. Some outsourcing providers have performed website templates, which the outsourcing team can personalize to the requirements of the company seeking outsourcing services. But this does not mean that all tasks related to web designing can be outsourced.

In a corporate set up where time is crucial, the standard web design requirements are best met with outsourcing. If the web designing needs substantial amount of innovation or creativity, which is especially the case for small business startups, hiring a web designer is essential. This way the designing can be monitored all through the lifecycle of the project.

Computer Programming

This is outsourced because it is similar to the accounting, tax and web design outsourcing services in having a standard format.

Programming projects such as setting up database, calculator, or message board are easily done by outsourcing services at relatively cheap rates.

While such run of the mill tasks can very well be outsourced, programming projects that are important for the entire business, and need concepts and knowledge, which only top level executives can handle should never be outsourced.

If this is not heeded, you can very well expect a low quality finished product due to improper knowledge, language barrier, and monitoring difficulties. On the other hand, when in house programmers are engaged, they are easy to monitor, communicate and the project will be more efficiently done, when compared to outsourcing the job to off shore workers.

Manufacturing

While earlier manufacturing was the most outsourced service in the US, now the trend has shifted to services such as telecom and finance. Nevertheless, manufacturing will remain one of the most commonly outsourced services due to many factors including the expenses of hiring locals including cost related to Medicare, unemployment, social security and others, which are not present when the tasks are outsourced elsewhere.

Data entry

Data entry jobs such as scanning, order processing, cataloging and indexing fit ideally into the outsourcing model. When a startup is looking to cut down costs, the best way is to outsource the data entry jobs.

But care should be taken to provide clear and precise instructions and definite deadlines. The level of accuracy in such jobs is quite good. Except in case of classified or sensitive data such as social security numbers or credit cards, other tasks are better done with outsourcing.

Research & Development

Financial research, customer demographics, market analysis, and pharmaceutical research can be taken care by off shore teams that have appropriate training in the specified field and in various methodologies. Since R&D is very important for the business to grow, and become established, finding the right outsourcing team that specializes in the field you require is important.

Legal Services

Services such as drafting, document review, litigation support, and legal documentation can be outsourced with confidence and you can easily save money this way. Other than defending in court, other legal details can be handled expertly by outsourcing. This is more so in case of small startups, which cannot afford the legal fees of large and reputed legal firms.

Creative tasks

Tasks such as advertising copy, logo design, content writing etc. can be handled adeptly by overseas firms. Such outsourcing services should be used, when you need the services only for a short time as hiring a full term employee is unnecessary for the temporary need.

Health care

This service includes tasks such as medical transcription, coding, medical billing, healthcare software, and tele radiology. Since sophisticated diagnostics and scanning needs have increased, they are more cost effective, when an overseas team takes over the tasks. But as with other outsourcing tasks such as accounting, medical information is very sensitive, so due care should be taken to outsource services of quality and reliable teams.

Engineering services

Engineering tasks including architectural, structural, electrical, and mechanical tasks and others can be done efficiently by outsourcing. Consulting, modelling, sketches, AutoCAD designs etc. can be done this way. Bust as in web design and computer programming, when the task is crucial, it is best to outsource only the standardized tasks and leave the innovative tasks to the executives in the company.

Common attributes that influence outsourcing

Some common factors that indicate the need for outsourcing include the following:

Tasks that need to be done, but you are unable to do them because of time constraints or if the tasks are annoying or boring, are perfect for outsourcing

Tasks that need not require perfection are good indicators for outsourcing. For instance, if you need information on a detail and you get 90 percent of the information via outsourcing it is more appropriate to use the outsourcing.

Tasks that have objective outcome such as those that depend on needs to be met with, instead of preferences are apt for outsourcing.

7. Places where you can get outsourcing assistance

Outsourcing is a preferred form of taking care of the operations of a company, as traditional workers do not guarantee good performance when compared to virtual outsourcing providers. Further, the flexibility in hiring as when the need arises is another advantage.

And the best benefit is acquiring top quality services at very low rates making it a very profitable solution, especially for a startup. For instance, a quality programmer in Silicon Valley would charge around $120 per hour, whereas if you outsource the job and get it done in Russia, Philippines, or India, it can be done around $20 per hour.

Therefore, the secret of a successful outsourcing lies in where you outsource your job. Here are some places where you can find excellent outsourcing providers related to any field. Each site mentioned here uses different layout, system, and project duration. You need to consider the competitive rates and quality results, while choosing the site for your outsourcing job.

Before you start visiting the sites, here are some things you will be required to do for selecting the outsourcing provider:

• Post the job description
• Receive proposals from prospective candidates
• Compare reviews, ratings, profiles, portfolios, credentials, and price

Here are some of the tops outsourcing sites found online:

Freelancer.com

This site works on milestone creation. Once milestones are completed, the employer releases payment. The fees include $5 refundable fee, which is refunded when you select a provider. For featured project, you need to pay $19 and $3 for selection of service provider. For full time projects, the site charges $99.95.

This site is good for work that is project based or on off tasks. The site is efficient and best for smaller projects. You can get an average job done here under $200, which makes outsourcing here a very cost effective solution for startups and small businesses.

Elance:

This site can be used to hire outsourcing providers, according to project or on hourly basis. You can later track your progress in the Workroom assigned for you. Screenshots, messages, completed work and files are saved here automatically. One beneficial feature here is you can invite coworkers to pitch in at the Workroom, when required.

Payment details involve timesheet or milestone approval, which are needed for making payment. As far as rates are concerned, a deduction ranging from 6.75 percent to 8.75 percent is done on each project, while the remaining amount is deposited in the Elance account of the service provider. Additionally a $10 activation fee for creating Employer account is charged as onetime fee.

In 2015, Elance and oDesk merged to form Upwork. You will find the top quality providers a bit expensive but this is a good choice, if you want to hire teams with technical expertise.

Upwork

When you outsource through this site you pay only for the time spent on the work you have assigned after verification. The Work Diary program of Upwork lets you see all the individual team members' mouse and keyboard activity, their feedback and screenshots and webcams too, so the workers are made more accountable.

Payment is based on completed tasks or hours worked. Fees charged include 10 percent of the payment made by the employer.

This site works best when you want to pay on hourly basis. Further Upwork had been formerly oDesk, which later merged in 2013 with Elance.

Guru

This site is based on payment for work completed. It focuses more on outsourcing providers based in the US. It has about 182,000 US workers, 51,242 Indian freelancers and 1887 Russian workers. For companies who need to work with native English speaking freelances this is a good option. And if your startup is looking for a provider based in the US, this is ideal.

Fees charged include 5 percent to 10 percent of the Escrow or invoice amount based on the membership level. Membership fees starts from $29.95 and extends to $99.95 for a quarter. Employer payment fees deduction includes 4% for credit card, 2.5 percent for withdrawal system, $3 for receiving funds via check, and for wire transfer payment of funds it is $9.

MTurk

This is part of Amazon with great functionality. It works based on splitting up a job into different parts and letting different people take care of the parts. This is an interesting approach and can work wonders, if it is appropriate for the requirements you have.

Team vs Individual outsourcing provider

You can choose between hiring teams or an individual worker. With individuals, you will know the person you are working with and create a good rapport with the working style of the person. You can also negotiate for a lower rate, while working directly. Control over the task and the person would be more, when compared to hiring a team or company. But with a company you will have advantages such as better skills, synergy, training and management. For long-term outsourcing, it is best to work with an individual.

Locations you should hire from

Here are some locations, which can give you the best outsourcing providers:

Russia, Ukraine, Belarus, and other countries belonging to erstwhile Soviet Union are good places for technically skilled coders Philippines has good marketers, writers, programmers, and researchers UK/USA/Canada has excellent providers, if you are looking for a particular field skill. Expats also are good choice as providers and you can find them easily in the expat forums. Choosing the right outsourcing site depends on the project you want to outsource. If it is hourly work, the perfect choice is Upwork. On the other hand, you want a one off task done, Freelancer.com and Guru are ideal. These sites have a proper payment and dispute handling systems, so the provider and employer are reassured. But most important part of outsourcing is having a clear-cut job description.

8. Making passive income a reality with outsourcing

Now that you have a detailed knowledge about outsourcing, and where to find the providers, you should move to the next aspect of outsourcing, which is management. Without proper management, earning passive income will be an out of reach dream only. The more focused you are on finding the right outsourcing and managing them, the better your profits will be.

But you need not worry. Since outsourcing is supposed to be a smart way of doing business where you work less and earn more, managing should be a breeze. If you were outsourcing just a single project, it would be child's play monitoring it. But when you have multiple projects to be taken care of you need to put in some efforts, so deadlines are respected and the work is up to the standards you want. Here are a few pointers to help you.

Motivate the providers

Overdue invoices, little or no communication, and ignoring complaints are things that you should avoid completely, if you expect the work to be of top quality and done on time. The best way to build a perfect working relationship with your outsourcing providers is to recognize their efforts, give positive feedback, and be prompt on the payment front.

Treat them as part of the business and if they are situated locally, invite them to company events and send them thank you cards and better still gifts that will make them feel happy that they are working for you. In short, if you treat them in a positive and friendly way, it will forge strong relationships and you will be able to get the best out of them. This will also help build a stronger bond in the long term, which is beneficial for both the business and the provider.

Instead of giving, a quick outline of the project and expecting top quality, try to give as much input as you can, so they have an exact idea of your expectations to act accordingly.

Rule of thumb:

One basic outsourcing rule you should never forget is forming a talent pool of providers who can deliver the quality you are looking for on time. When you expand this team into a larger one over time, your work will be much easier and would be done smoothly without any hitches. Here are some basic rules you should remember while outsourcing

• Decide on the aspects you want to focus on in your business and the activities that could be outsourced in an efficient and cost effective way, and find the appropriate outsourcing providers.

• Create proper agreements that detail all your expectations and that of the outsourcing service.

• Make sure you communicate constantly. This will ensure the work is done according to your requirements.

• Since outsourcing providers work for several teams at a time, to ensure your work is done effectively, you need to monitor the work continuously. Quality work and prompt delivery can be guaranteed this way.

Equip for emergencies

Even the best-planned projects can go wrong some way or the other. Sometimes, the regular provider may not deliver your work on time, or of the quality, you need. You may have to hire another individual, at a higher price too, to get the work done. To ensure your business continues operating smoothly, you should not make assumptions that everything would happen as you had planned.

Always have a backup method in case things go wrong. Have a system to fall back on during emergencies. Have plenty of time for a project and get it finished well before the deadline, so if anything goes wrong, you have the time to hire another provider to finish the work.

As mentioned before outsourcing is not for all businesses. Your business can benefit from outsourcing when it can capably provide the experience, expertise, and skills your business needs in a cost effective way.

In the highly competitive global marketplace, you need to have a shared vision, adaptability, and flexibility to ensure a performance oriented business. A good outsourcing team, proper back up system, ability to minimize issues and negative impact of the issues are necessary, if you want to keep that passive income flowing in.

Conclusion

While startups embark on their business confident in their skills being sufficient to drive the business, they cannot do everything. This overenthusiasm can only stall the business growth. Outsourcing routine tasks and tasks that need specialized skills will help entrepreneurs to focus on the task of generating profits.

Outsourcing as you would have realized by now is a wise strategy that can give the impetus a startup needs. The technological developments of today have made it easier to find good outsourcing providers enabling businesses including small firms to fast track their growth, bottom lines and productivity.

Outsourcing has become an integral part of how businesses function as the present day business atmosphere enables professionals to work from almost any place and be readily accessible. You can now find some of the top professionals, marketing directors, executive virtual assistants, graphic designers, paralegals, transcriptionists, web designers, IT experts, PR specialist, bookkeepers, and others easily accessible.

With time and money consuming issues such as overheads, taxes, insurance, and compensation being avoided with outsourcing along with the elimination of space requirements, startups can grow uninhibitedly and make giant strides in their business in a very short span, when compared to developing an in-house business.

While the initial few steps in outsourcing may look overwhelming, when you know the way to proceed, and the pitfalls to look for, you can easily build your startup into a business with growing efficiency and productivity. Since you relegate all the essential tasks that you cannot work on personally to professional outsourcing providers, you will be able to compete with the bigger players easily and win.

The ideal time to take up outsourcing depends on the business. Some companies have staff to take care of the daily activities and need outsourcing to deal with any new projects for which they may have to hire new staff to look after.

Another scenario is, when the normal activities are unable to be managed by the current employees and this is becoming a hurdle for your business. In such an instance, your business may face serious setbacks. If you want your business to develop, delegating work via outsourcing is the sure fire way to increase the revenue manifold.

Startups can outsource right from the beginning. A virtual assistant and bookkeeper to begin with and later on a team of outsourcing providers would be a good and profitable way to develop the startup. As highlighted in this book, any type of task, complex and simple, can be outsourced with success.

But at the same time remember to take care of the core aspects of your business on your own as these tasks are critical for your business and your contribution is necessary. When you adhere to this concept and ensure you follow the outsourcing guidelines explained in this book, a steady stream of passive income will be possible with your startup.

Best of luck!